Memories of Company C

The World War I Memoir of John S. Hubert

Co. C, 2nd Engineer Regiment, 2nd Division, A.E.F.

Edited by James P. Gregory, Jr.

STORIED
publishing
edited
something
storied.pub

ISBN: 978-1-951991-30-2

Edited by Doug Serven

Cover design by Sean Benesh

Published by Storied Publishing

Editor's Note

John Stephen Hubert was born on September 10, 1901, to Theodore and Clara Hubert in Chicago, Illinois. On April 24, 1917, he joined the United States Army at the age of 15. He successfully lied about his age and found himself placed in the 2nd Engineer Regiment. As a part of that unit, he would serve as a runner in some of the fiercest battles with the 2nd Division, American Expeditionary Forces that nearly cost him his life multiple times. This includes inhaling mustard gas, for which he was awarded the Purple Heart Medal.

Fortunately for us all, John survived the war and wrote this memoir. Thanks to his work, this is one of the only known written accounts from a member of the 2nd Engineers during World War I. This work is one of remembrance and love from a veteran who did not want the men he served alongside to be forgotten in history. Nor did he want anyone to forget the great sacrifice many of his generation made when they served in France.

Written in the late 1970s, Hubert's sharp memory provides a unique perspective of the role of not only the 2nd Engineers but also of runners who braved snipers, bombardments, and poison gas to deliver messages to and from the frontlines. Hubert also included a discussion of his life after the war as he and other veterans struggled to find their place back in society. The formation of veteran groups like the American Legion helped the men reconnect and find some camaraderie as they shared their struggles and memories of the war.

In the final chapter of this book, Hubert shares the story of his return to France in 1971 with his wife, Esther. During this trip, he visited the towns and battlegrounds he had traversed fifty-three years prior. This trip stirred many memories for Hubert, especially when visiting the graves of his friends who had fallen during the war. As he said in a 1981 interview, "I can remember more of 1918, 1919, and 1920 than I can remember what happened six months ago. You don't help pick up a man in pieces and forget about it."[1] It was those memories that drove him to work on this book from 1978–1980.

Once John had finished his book, he self-published it, only printing thirty copies. These were sent to veterans he had served with, their relatives, and various organizations, such as the American Battle Monuments Commission.

Once his work was completed, John kept up his fulfilling life, pursuing his hobby of prospecting until he passed away on January 31, 1996. He is buried in Dearborn Memorial Park, Poway, California.

It would not be until 2021, when I received a PDF of this work by WWI 2nd Division Historian and Archivist Steven C. Girard, that I was made aware of Hubert's story. I quickly realized the significance of the story and tracked down his family. They graciously sent me the original draft of Hubert's memoir full of photos and pasted maps.

Hubert also wrote several smaller stories about his life after the war that were not distributed which I have included in this book. To ensure that all men were given their credit, in cases where John has used a nickname for a fellow veteran, I have added a footnote with the full name of the individual. This work provides not only a fascinating look at the 2nd Engineers and their role in the conflict, but it also gives us a look at the long-term complications from poison gas and the quest for understanding after such a terrible war.

---

1. David Hart, "Armistice Day has Special Meaning for RB Vet," *Times-Advocate*, Escondido, California, November 11, 1981.

By John C. Hubert

About a year ago, I read an article that emphasized the need to forget yesterday and last year, stating that the brain has a limited capacity and one should leave room for today and tomorrow. Well, at 78, I realize that there are not too many tomorrows left for me, and I like to remember parts of the past, the yesterdays of long ago, and the many friends that were part of and contributed to those memories. Most of those memories are happy ones that I cherish. When an old army friend and I get together, and they are old now, we have a session of "Do you remembers?" The sad ones and fearful ones I try to forget but down deep I cannot.

My mother passed away in 1934 when I was 32. Esther and I had been married a few months earlier while I was on a prolonged visit to Chicago. At the funeral parlor, we were introduced to relatives of my mother, people that I had no memory of. One lady commented at our introduction, "Oh, you are the boy who ran away." This sort of startled me since it came from someone who was a stranger to me. It started the memory wheel rolling.

Yes, I guess I did run away. I ran away from something, or did I run towards something? I did not run away from home because at that time I was living with former neighbors, paying for room and board. My father had died when I was 8 due to an accident, and when I was 15, my mother decided to live with my older sister. I graduated from grammar school prior to my 15th birthday, and it was necessary for me to go to work in order to earn enough to pay my own way. In my youthful years, I loved to read the paperbacks of those days about Buffalo Bill and other notorious characters of the Wild West. So in the early spring of 1917, I ran away from my monotonous job, and I boarded a train from Chicago. I decided to go west and be a cowboy and see the many wonderful places that I had read about.

During the spring of 1966, while on a visit to northern Illinois, we drove through Mendota, stopped, and visited an old friend, Theodore Becker. Later I drove to Dyer, Indiana, to visit another old army friend, James Higgins. We had not seen each other since 1919. Jim was like an older brother to me. Everybody liked Ted and Jim and always had pleasant memories of them. Our conversations again awakened memories. I will write more about them later.

In the fall of 1971, after a tour of Europe, Esther and I were able to visit Belleau Wood and the cemetery there. This again brought back memories, some sad ones. These memories pushed me to write this book.

Chapter 1

Co. C at Home

Shortly after war was declared, I was in Denver, Colorado. Noticing a group of men walking towards the railroad station with their suitcases, I wandered over to the entrance of the establishment that they had come out of, which proved to be a recruiting office. While I was standing there, a sergeant came out and questioned me about my age. He said, "You know, a couple of days ago, Congress passed a bill saying that you could enlist at eighteen without your parents' consent." I said, "They did?"

I noticed Uncle Sam on a poster pointing his finger at me, with the words "I want you." I said, "Well, I'm eighteen." He said, "Well you look 18 to me." So, as a result, I was shipped to Fort Logan, Colorado where after going through numerous physical checks and tests, it was found that I stood 5'4" and weighed 112 pounds, which was twenty pounds under the minimum limit.

However, while checking my heart and lungs, the doctor trapped me into admitting my right age which was fifteen. He patted me on the backside and said, "OK, I'll keep your secret." So I was sworn in.

After getting several more shots, my uniform, and other

instructions, I was shipped off to Camp Baker which was about five miles north of El Paso, Texas. I became a member of the 5th, who were camped across the highway from the 2nd Engineers where we were to be trained.

After about 10 days of preliminary instructions, I explained to the sergeant in charge of us that I knew all of the marching drills and that manual of arms, and upon questioning, I told him that I knew most of the silent manual. I had learned these drills as a member of St. Mary's Cadets, an organization sponsored by the Paulist Fathers of St. Mary's Cathedral on the south side of Chicago. Bill Wahler, Bill Smith, Jack Fogle, and I, classmates at our Lady of Lourdes parochial school had been members during the seventh and eighth grades.[1] As a result of this bragging, I was transferred to the 2nd Engineers, across the road.

There, under the supervision of Corporal John Vickers, new arrivals, or recruits, were to receive additional training before assignment to various platoons in the regular company. I became acquainted with a group who had come in from Fort Slocum, New York. There was David Jones from Plymouth, Pennsylvania, Stanley Weber from Long Island, Bill Lander, Arthur Chaplin, and Bill Checkley from New Jersey.[2] These were my early friends, and they remained so as long as they lived.

Corporal Vickers taught Dave and me how to use semaphore flags and to be able to send messages with them.

We were to be runners or messengers. After we got to France, we never saw a semaphore flag again.

On my first day with C Company of the 2nd Engineers, I lined up with the rest of the Company at the dinner meal time, and as I approached the food counter, Jim Sheridan, one of the cooks on duty, piped up with, "Look at the chicken. Feed him up men. Let's make a man out of him."[3] My response, I am told, was of a nature that I hesitate to repeat here. I guess this is what caused some to picture me as hard-boiled. Well, I wasn't. I was just trying to keep these older fellows from getting too many funny ideas. The name "Chick" stuck with me for the rest of my time with C Company.

Corporal John L. Vickers (left) John Hubert (right)

We were moved over to the Company after a couple of weeks. Lizards and horned toads were plentiful as was the cactus in the area where we drilled. The temperature stayed at 110 for three straight weeks. When we were drilling to silent signals, the officers were not aware of the locations of the cactus in front of you. They expected you to fall into a prone position when they gave the signal to do so. I could never do this, so I was scolded several times.

There was Sergeant Charlie Bussle, who had seven or eight years of service before World War I. He was quite a gambler and ladies' man. Each payday evening, Charlie set up a table at the end of the company street and would run a crap game. After my first payday, Charlie, showing me how to do it, would turn the game over to me to run after the first night or if he had a date. He also taught me how to handle dice and how to evenly roll them. When he would turn the game over to me to run, I would have a few extra dollars as my share of the cut.

During this summer period, we were taken to the rifle range to practice so we would know how to handle a gun when we shot for record. During the practice at the base of Mt. Franklin, my record was that of a sharpshooter. But on the first shot, several of the fellows were standing watching me to see what would happen. They got quite a bang out of what happened. The kick from the rifle pushed me down the slope 6 or 8 inches. When it came time to shoot for record, I shot marksman but failed in estimating distances from where we were standing to certain objects in the landscape. It was so hot, heat waves seemed to make things move up and down.

Then there was the incident of getting my medicinal shots again. I had had all of my shots that were scheduled, but somewhere along the line in the transfers from the 5th Engineers, these records went missing. So since there were not six weeks left for me to have a shot each Saturday, I was given two shots each time. The first time that I was given the two, there was a big fellow almost twice my size standing behind me waiting his turn and watching. When the second needle was stuck into my arm, he fainted.

On August 22, 1917, the Regiment left Camp Baker by rail. We stopped along the way. It took us five days to get to our destination, we had to make way for through trains. We stopped at Bay St. Louis on the Gulf, where the fellows were allowed to go swimming. We stopped in New Orleans for several hours, and some of the men went to one of the pleasure districts to have some fun. Since I was not acquainted with that type of fun, my friends discouraged me from accompanying them.

Several of us walked and looked over the portion of the city near the station. We arrived in Washington D.C. and were quartered in tents on the grounds of the American University. While in Washington, we saw all of the sights. I walked up the stairs of the Washington Monument, equal to twenty stories. On another day, I rode up and walked down. The day before we left, we paraded on Pennsylvania Ave. past the Capitol Building and marched in review for President Woodrow Wilson.

Early on the morning of September 10th, my sixteenth birthday, we entrained for New York, where we boarded a

British troop transport named the "Good Ship," *Carpathia*. It received that name due to having come to the rescue where the Titanic was sunk. We arrived in Halifax the next day. Having missed our scheduled convoy, we had to lay in the harbor for nine more days waiting for the gathering of another convoy.

The only break in the monotonous wait was to tie a handkerchief at the four corners, attach a long string or twine, and try to haul up a jellyfish, there were many floating in the harbor. Fun?

We finally left Halifax and after eleven days, we reached Glasgow, Scotland. We were met a day out by American destroyers which crisscrossed through the convoy of about twenty ships to make sure none of them would be torpedoed by German submarines. From Glasgow, we took a train to South Hampton, England.

---

1. Jack Fogle is LeRoy G. Fogle.
2. Bill Lander is William D. Lander and Bill Checkley is William T. Checkley Jr.
3. Jim Sheridan is James L. Sheridan

Chapter 2

Colombey-les-Belles to Longeau

We spent three days in South Hampton, and while we were there, we were a curiosity to many people, especially the young ladies. They had never seen an American soldier before, dressed with campaign hats upon which there was a cord with knobs at the end that resembled acorns. The Engineers, of course, had a red and white striped hat cord and the girls would come up to us and ask for a cherry off our hat. At least that is what I thought that they were referring to. At the end of three days, we boarded a ferry-type ship that was propelled by large paddle wheels, one on each side. The English Channel was quite rough that night and quite a few got seasick.

We arrived at La Havre, France. Here we were to start a new experience, traveling in boxcars, much small than the ones we were familiar with in America. Instead of a truck with four wheels at each end, there were only two wheels at each end. They carried a sign on each side which, when interpreted, said forty men or eight horses.

Company C was sent to Colombey-les-Belles, which we always referred to as Colombey. This village of about three-hundred population was located about twenty-four kilometers south of the city of Nancy, in the Provence of Lorraine. We were assigned to billets, the hay lofts of the farmhouses where we spread our blankets on the loose hay. The houses all faced the road and were built close to or against each other. There was a common entrance in front of each structure; the cattle and farm equipment occupied one side and the residents the other. You could tell who was the wealthiest farmer by the size of the manure pile located out in front of the building. This was standard for all of the farm villages in this part of France.

Colombey-les-Belles farmhouse.
2nd floor billet, in hayloft.
As it looks today. Taken 1971.

The cafe at the turn of the road.
Colombey-les-Belles.

After being in Colombey a few days, Paddy O'Gorman, who had gone to bed a little tipsy, had to get up during the night. Being a little dizzy, he missed the ladder, and since there was no guard rail around it, he fell out of the loft.[1] Paddy went to the hospital and never returned to the company. I did run into him years later in 1932 at Edward Hines Veterans Hospital, which is located in Maywood,

Illinois. We had quite a visit. He was amazed that I still remembered him and commented that in the intervening years I had grown up and changed to the point that he did not recognize me.

After being stationed in Colombey for a couple of weeks, the company was moved to Bairsey-au-Plain. Shortly after this move, a part of the company was sent to Vaucoulours. Eighteen of us returned to Colombey to work under the direction of a Master Electrician of the Signal Corps. At that time, the Signal Corps was in charge of our air force. We unloaded cantonments which came in assembled sections. We unloaded rails and tiles for the extension of the railroad which would serve the first American airfield. They would slide rails down from the flat cars and the Master Electrician would give us instructions by singing out, "Lay your hands on it, pick it up, move it away."

About a dozen men would follow these instructions and move the rail to the truck that would snake away three rails at a time. My job was to put a chain through a hole in the rail, lock it, and when we got to the truck, loop the chain over a hook on the back of the truck. Then when it arrived at the point of storage, I would reverse the procedure. It was the easiest job I ever had.

The café at the head of the street was a meeting place when we had a few francs. We gathered there and some of the fellows would sing, and on occasions, French airmen would drop in from a nearby airfield, and there would be a blending of harmony. Once in a while, we would get involved in a dice game on the billiard table. I won over a hundred dollars for the first time. The major portion that time was lost by the Master Electrician who liked to join in on our activities. We always accepted him as one of us.

Shortly after we arrived in France, we learned that we were to be a unit of the 2nd Division, U.S. Regular Army. Of the two infantry brigades, one, the Third Brigade, consisting of the 9th and 23rd Infantry, had sailed or were preparing to do so. The 4th Brigade was to be a brigade of Marines. The 5th Marines, then in France as part of the 1st Division, and the 6th Marines were in the process of organizing at Quantico, Virginia, as was the 6th Machine Gun Battalion. The artillery brigade had the 12th, the 15th, and the 17th Regiments, which were preparing to leave. We, the 2nd Engineers, were in France. The other units assigned as part of the Division, were on their way or preparing to leave America.

General Omar Bundy, then in France, was designated as Division Commander. The Division was assembled beginning in October 1917 in the training area in and around the city of Bourmont. The 6th Marines and the 6th Machine Gun Battalion joined the division after the first of the year, 1918.

After a short time, we returned to headquarters at Bairsey-au-Plain where we were occupied in the building of a hospital. It rained a great deal of the time, and we worked in knee-deep mud for which they furnished us with hip boots. About the first of December, C Company, E Company, and Headquarters moved to Longeau.

Boy, was it cold; the snow on the ground creaked when you walked on it. We arrived about 5:00 a.m. We made a beeline for a café nearby, got a woman up about 5:30, and asked for something warm to drink, thinking about coffee. I was amazed and delighted after the first sip. It was Rumchaud or hot rum, my first experience with rum and hot coffee.

When we left the United States, our strength for each company was 165 men. It was decided while we were en route that the number would be increased and the companies replaced to a strength of 250 men. These replacements were sent to Longeau, where Headquarters was stationed. About one-third of these new men had served in the National Guard. Two-thirds were draftees who at the time of joining the Regiment were of short service and lacked some training. They had come to us from the 116th Engineers, which had become a replacement unit.

Great efforts were made to give these men proper training, but it was not as thorough as desired. During the later portion of the time the companies were on construction work, one hour's drill per day, close order if possible, was prescribed to keep the men in hand. These orders could not be carried out thoroughly in all companies, but the results were good when followed.

Two incidents that are very clear in my mind today occurred at Longeau. It had got to the point in a dice game that when it was my turn to shoot, it was difficult sometimes to get someone to fade my bets. They were afraid of me. We had two visitors in the café one night, a sergeant and a corporal from E. Co. Both were noted gamblers. I had lost what little money I had by fading some other fellows.

Bill Lander and Cleon Dawson had come into the café and were standing behind me. So when it came to my turn, Bill said, "Are you going to shoot, Chick?" I told him that I was broke, so he laid twenty francs on the table and said, "Chick shoots twenty francs." I made a pass, and Bill said, "He shoots forty francs." The sergeant from E Co. got on my money and followed through on the fourth pass when I was shooting 160 francs.

He caught my dice eleven times; he stopped them. After the eleventh time in a row, I told him to get off my money or leave the dice alone. He said, "Alright." I then proceeded to make the most perfect even roll of my entire army life. The sergeant quit in disgust, and Bill and I divided the money. We each had 160 francs. No one else would follow through by fading my bet. The blankets on the table were too smooth, and my rolling was too even.

On my way to my billet, I stopped where there was a

poker game going on. Jim Higgins was playing, and he invited me to sit down and asked me how things were going.[2] I told him what had happened, and he said, "Do you want to play poker?" I had never played poker in the service for money. I knew the fundamentals of the game so he invited me to sit next to him, and as we went along, he coached me. I think I left the place five or ten francs on the losing side, but I had a good time.

Christmas came along, and we did not have our turkey for the Holiday. We had been expecting turkey, but somehow the shipment went awry, and we did without. But it was bitter cold. It had kicked up a storm, and there was a lot of snow on the ground.

Longeau lay eleven kilometers south of Langres along the highway north of Dijon. This was the highway, as I was told, that Caesar's army made during the invasion of Gaul. Langres was a city built with three walls, moats, and draw bridges encircling the city. It was a city of good size, and on the several occasions that we visited there, we enjoyed the trip. I was especially interested in the feature of the walls and draw bridges and that it was located on Caesar's Highway.

In between Christmas and New Year, we left Longeau and moved to Sauville in the Bourmont area. The move was again made by the forty eight box cars. At Sauville, we were to go through intensive training. When we detrained, we got out into bitter cold weather. We had been traveling all night, stopping here and waiting there for the right of way. Since we were forty men and our equipment in a French box car, we were pretty well bundled together, and we managed to stay fairly warm. When we got out of the cars, the snow creaked under our feet when we walked on it. We had breakfast. One box car had a temporary kitchen set up in it. We then set off on a four-kilometer hike into the town of Sauville. For the New Year of 1918, we had a double load of turkey for dinner.

---

1.   Paddy O'Gorman is David O'Gorman.
2.   Jim Higgins is James P. Higgins.

Chapter 3

Sauville to Bar-le-Duc

T he Regiment continued on construction work until the companies were relieved on various dates from December 30th to January 14th. When the entire Regiment had been assembled in the area about Bourmont, headquarters for the 2nd Division, it went into training as part of that Division. Headquarters Company and the 2nd Battalion were at Vrecourt, the First Battalion was at Sauville, and the Engineer Train was at Rozieres-Sur-Mouzon. Then followed the longest and almost the only real training that the regiment had since arriving in France, with that of the First Battalion lasting until February 26th, and for the Second Battalion and Headquarters lasting until March 14th.

In this area, the homes and farmhouses that were part of this small city were different than our previous experiences. I recall only a few manure piles, and we no longer slept in hay lofts. We were given unfurnished upper floors. We used straw-filled bed ticks to sleep on. This community appeared to be the center of activity for a great area and was large enough to house the entire First Battalion. Of course, within the bounds of each company area, there would be a café, and generally, these cafés became the evening meeting place for the men.

This did not mean that all of us would drink alcoholic beverages. If we did, it would generally be a light wine or beer. Some just visited.

The café that C Company utilized for its gatherings was situated in the center of the billeting area. We had not received our pay during December; we were waiting patiently to get our hands on some money. I found out that Jim Higgins had got credit at the café with assistance from Jack Dillon.[1] It seems that Dillon, a Sgt. 1st Class, was billeted in one of the bedrooms at the café. The old café owner was also the baker and he would get up at four or five in the morning and go to the bakery, and on occasion when he did, I was informed, his young wife would crawl into bed with Dillon. So Dillon stood pretty good. When Jim told me that he had got credit, I went to Dillon and prevailed on him to get me credit. So Jim and I were the ones who on occasion until we were paid, bought the wine for our group.

About a week after New Year's, I received a Christmas package from home. A wooden box. I had written to my brother Nick previously and had asked him, if it was possible, to send me some American-made dice because the French dice all had rounded corners, pretty difficult to even roll dice like this. In the package I received, there was a knit sweater, a knit helmet for the bad winter, knit gloves, a box of fudge that my sister Agnes had made (she was really good at making fudge), a box of cookies, three decks of playing cards, and three sets of dice. It was a pleasure too to get the American playing cards. With the help of others in the family, Nick had been very thoughtful in preparing this Christmas remembrance. At this time, no one else had received a package from Christmas yet, so all of my friends and others were interested and wanted to help me enjoy it.

On February 27th, the 1st Battalion was detached from the Regiment and sent to the front north of Toul. This area was occupied by the 1st Division, and we were to supplement the 1st Engineers. They were engaged in work at the engineer dump, sawmills, and in the construction of shelters on lines in the rear. Their work was in such locations that they suffered no casualties.

The First battalion was sent to Boucq, which was a pleasant little city situated in the hill country. We were there for a short period when Company A was sent to Menil-la-Tour. Company B remained at Boucq, and Company C was sent to Sanzey. Company A operated engineer dumps; Company C constructed the greater part of the Army dump at Leonval, involving the construction of wagon and truck roads and standard gauge railways, warehouses, and platforms, built a stable at Sanzey, and did concrete work at Fort Gironville. Company B remained at Boucq, operated sawmills and assisted in the construction work at Leonval. During this period, each company made necessary repairs and improvements to bridges and roads throughout the sector. On May 9th, 1918, the First Battalion moved by truck to Heiltz-le-Maurupt along the Marne where it rejoined the 2nd Division for duty.

During its stay in this sector near Bar-le-Duc, the 2nd Engineers were engaged in training and railhead and remount work for the 2nd Division. The German drives of March and April caused conditions to become quite serious, and the 2nd Division was needed near Paris. The First Division was preparing to win the battle at Cantigny on May 28, and it was decided that the 2nd Division could help in that vicinity. Accordingly, the tour of trenches was discontinued and the whole Division was assembled from May 10th to 12th for rest and training in the vicinity of Bar-le-Duc. Here we spent about eight days cleaning up, equipping, drilling, rifle firing, etc., in a beautiful part of the country, with the idea that we were bound for the Somme.

We then moved by rail and then three days of terrific hiking. I say terrific because the Major was the only one riding a horse and because the weather had turned extremely warm, quite a few men fell out on the hike because they could not keep up with the horse. The Major was angry about this, so on the second day, he increased the gait. Along about halfway on the second day, my nose started to bleed, and it happened that the medical Lieutenant was walking right alongside me saw the blood and ordered me to fall out, and when the wagons came along to put my pack on the wagon and march behind it. That pack and equipment we carried was rated at ninety pounds, and the Major rode a horse and did not carry a pack. The other officers walked, but their gear was in the wagon.

It happened that Louis Kumpf was also ordered to put his pack on the wagon when it came along and caught up with us. We wandered down into the town which lay below the highway. There was a café close by which we went into. Kumpf told me that he had only one franc. I had five so we were sure of at least one drink of rum, which we felt would make us feel better. Of course, they were served in small glasses, and the woman asked for five sous apiece. This was equal to a five-cent piece in our money. So we had a couple apiece.

Then we went back to the highway, and shortly the wagons came along. We put our packs on C Company's ration cart, and we walked on behind. Things were easier the next day. I think someone had worked on the Major since he was doing us more harm than good.

We soon arrived at Caumont-et-Vixen which was northwest of Paris. Here a week was used for training and on Decoration Day orders came that changed the whole picture. The Second Division was diverted to the Chateau-Thierry front to stop the German drive in that direction. How we stopped them will be shown in the next chapter.

Before going into our journey to the Chateau-Thierry front, I want to go back to our stay at Sanzey and the work we did in the woods at Leonval. We had two sergeants who were considered pretty tough, hard men to get along with. We thought they were drivers. Of course, they had been in the service several years, and I guess they were just dedicated men. Sergeant Harvey Silverstone and Sergeant Edwin Waltman. Silverstone left us about this time to go to officer training school. We had been busy, and I had been detailed to help dig a roadbed for the laying of railroad tracks into the wood. We had cut trees and performed other duties about this project, and one morning I was part of a detail sent to unload cinders to be used as ballast.

The lieutenant, who I was not familiar with, sat on the brake wheel at the end of the flat car and watched us as we shoveled the cinders over the side. The scoop that I had was pretty heavy; I would have been satisfied just using the empty scoop. After shoveling for a while, I straightened out. My back was tired and ached. I sort of stretched a little bit and the lieutenant piped up, "All right Private Hubert, keep on shoveling. Take it easy, but keep on shoveling."

The next morning when the detail halted to go on with shoveling, I kept on going for four kilometers, back to the town of Boucq. I stopped at a café that had been our headquarters, ordered a glass of vin blanc, and had drank about half of it when in walked Waltman.

Sergeant Waltman said, "I thought I would find you here. Come on, get going." He would not let me finish the glass of wine. So I had to go back to the construction site. He walked me back and made sure that I was going to do some more shoveling. Nothing else happened after that in the way of punishment except some kitchen police duty. I just sort of hated him.

Later, on the hike to Chaumont-en-Vixen, on the second night of that three-day hike, Ed Waltman had been invited by a couple of the fellows to join them for a drink at a café, and he accepted, something that he had never done before. In the year that I had known him, he has never associated with fellows in a café. He had a couple of drinks with the boys, and the next day they reported that he was a very good sport; he was just a real fellow. From then on, it seemed like the difference between night and day. Sergeant Waltman acted more like a human being. I don't know whether he had a premonition of something to come or if he was acting like his real self.

———————————————

1. Jack Dillon is John M. Dillon.

Chapter 4

Chateau Thierry – Belleau Wood

A lthough the Division had made its tour of trench warfare in the quiet sectors (I say "quiet" because from Verdun to the Vosges Mountains was considered quiet sectors in 1918, where the French troops rested) the Americans got their first experience in the front lines without any general warfare. Night raids to determine strength in the units involved were made; in some instances, prisoners were taken; and some casualties were experienced. This condition prevailed after the great battle at Verdun when the German Crown Prince lost almost a million men in his attempt to capture that city and its fortifications. Verdun and Pont-a-Musson became the hinge of the St. Mihiel salient, which was in a cup shape. The area was mountainous, and the enemy had never been able to penetrate further. The lower portion of this cup shape salient extended a few miles west of St. Mihiel. Although stationed close to the front line, the First Battalion did not experience any trench duties until later and then while resting and retraining.

Now we were about to experience a new adventure. At 8 p.m. we received instructions to pack all of our gear and be prepared to move out. That evening, we marched to a highway four kilometers from our billets and assembled with the rest of the Regiment. The trucks that were to move us, however, did not arrive until the next morning at ten o'clock.

We waited all night; the entire Division was on the move. The trucks were light, French-made; the drivers of trucks that we rode in, mainly were from French Indo-China, Anamites. We were packed in pretty tight; the drivers drove like madmen.

We were aware later when we watched the sun that we were not on our way to relieve the 1st Division at Cantigny. We were held up for a while at Meaux due to German planes bombing that city, but where were *we* headed?

The road was almost blocked by trucks loaded with men, trucks loaded with ammunition and supplies, and refugees headed in the direction of Paris with as much of their belongings as they could out onto a two-wheel cart which was pulled by a horse or a couple of oxen, or in some instances pulled by the fleeing people themselves. The bombardment at Meaux lasted for about a half hour, and then the convoy quickly moved forward again. At about 5 a.m. the next morning we arrived at May-en-Multien. The Regiment unloaded, but it was found that several trucks had not arrived, so we fell out and waited until 6 o'clock. All of the regiment was then accounted for so we moved out.

We arrived at Montreuil-aux-Lions about noon. We had traveled all night and, having been up all of the previous night, we were pretty tired. Camp was made in a nearby field. The retreating French soldiers had their kitchens with them, and they gave us their food and coffee until their kettles were empty.

A strange incident occurred. We were having a prolonged rest break, sitting in a field away from and lower than the highway. Marines went by on the road and I saw one who looked just like Jack Fogle, a former eighth-grade classmate.[1] I tried to attract his attention but failed. I had received a letter from a friend a short time previous, telling me that Jack had enlisted in the Marine Corps and was at Quantico, Virginia, so it could not be him. I was to find out later that it was him.

On the 15th of June, two weeks later, at Bouresches, his arm was shattered just above the wrist, and the war was over for him. He was so close to me for several months, and I did not know it. He was one of my best friends.

We learned as we hurried forward that we were

heading in the direction of Chateau-Thierry. The French regiments who were retreating, going back while we were going forward, told us that nothing could stop the Bosch, a name that they had for the Germans. Some of these Frenchmen were going home on leave which was overdue. Many of them expressed the opinion that they did not care who won, just so it ended. They were tired of war, and there we were, rushing into something that they were running away from. One of the hardships of this forced marching for two hours without a rest was the fact that, in addition to our regulation heaving marching order pack and other equipment, each engineer carried a pick or shovel on the back of his pack. And in addition, each of us carried eight to ten bandoliers of ammunition. Each bandolier held sixty 30-caliber bullets.

Company C had orders to report to the Commanding Officer of the 23rd Infantry and do engineer duty with that Regiment. The 1st and 4th platoons were assigned to the 1st battalion of the 23rd Regiment, while the 2nd and 3rd platoons were assigned to the 3rd battalion of the infantry regiment. These battalions assisted in the repulse of the attack made by the enemy. Company C was the right company in the attack on June 6th. Orders were received by C company to go into action as the 4th wave, carrying entrenching tools to dig in when the objective was reached. As ordered, they went over as the 4th wave, but casualties were heavy in all of the waves. By the time they reached the first wave, no infantry officers were left. So the engineers with their remaining officers carried the line to its objective until relieved by other infantry that night.

During the day, I was with a special detail, fairly close to one of the Marine attacking forces. As we approached a wooded area close to Bouresches, we observed a Marine crawling on the ground in our direction. The corporal in charge of my squad was assigned, with his men, to help this wounded leather-neck to a first aid station. Two men would lock hands and wrists to make a seat and thus carry the wounded.

As we went around one section of the wood we came upon a second Marine crawling out of the trees, the brother of the first one assisted. While the other members of my squad took turns carrying the brothers, I carried the rifles of those assisting. This particular incident has always been embedded in my mind. One of the wounded brothers had been hit in one of his hips, the other had a piece of shrapnel in his lower abdomen. Instead of complaining about pain, they laughingly kidded each other about being so careless.[2]

After leaving the first aid station, we rejoined our platoon. That night, the front line was established, Belleau Wood to Triangle Farm and through La Rochette Woods. After being relieved from holding the front line, Company C set to work on the position of principal resistance near Triangle Farm, remaining there strengthening positions

until June 18th, when it was ordered to return to La
Croisette Wood to rejoin the 1st Battalion. Companies A
and B were assigned to similar duties with other infantry
regiments. The 2nd Battalion was assigned to duty with
the Marine Brigade.

One of the assignments we had after June 6th was to
dig graves for the dead. I believe it was June 7th. The detail
I was on worked in one corner of La Rochette Wood. We
dug graves wide enough to hold eight bodies, three feet
deep with an extra foot and a half of depth where each
body would lie. We got thirsty; it was quite warm that day,
and the fellows asked if I could go and get some water and
fetch some canteens. In passing some of the men of my
platoon, I was told that Orra L. Snyder, one of our buglers,
had been killed. A six-inch shell had exploded in the trees,
and the nose of the shell had buried into his back while he
was sitting on the outside of his dugout. When I returned
to the grave digging detail, I told them about Snyder, and
they told me, "Chick, while you were gone a shell landed
almost where you were working, and it killed Georgie
Godwin." George was a particularly good friend of mine.

About midnight on the night of the 7th, all hell broke
loose. Shells were exploding in the tree tops. I woke up,
crawled out of my dugout, and found the sky aflame with
flares. Shells were coming from the enemy, and our
artillery was firing over us at the enemy. It was frightening.
Machine guns in the open area to the rear of us were firing

at the enemy, and this was one of the two times that I could say I was really frightened.

With artillery and machine guns firing from the back of us and the enemy firing from the front, I thought the company had moved out during the night and had left me behind. I reached over and into the next dugout, found and woke up David Jones; he was still sleeping. We stood there for a few seconds and watched the brilliant display. wWhen there was a couple of seconds lull, Davie said, practical as he always was, "Well, let's wait until morning, Chick, then we will find out." With that we went back to sleep. In the morning, we found that the Germans were making a counterattack, that our artillery was responding, and machine guns in the rear of us, in reserve, were firing in the general direction of the enemy. It was during this counterattack that my friend Bill Checkley, also Rollin Freshour and Arthur Woodman, were wounded and taken prisoner. Their platoon was in a different part of the wood and closer to the enemy. I have very fond memories of Bill Checkley and his many kind tokens of friendship.

The second battalion of our regiment had had a rough time supporting, fighting with, and putting up barbwire in front of their positions for the Marine Brigade at Bouresches and after they had effected a foothold in Belleau Wood. On June 18, we were ordered back to La Coisette Wood. From then on, through the balance of June, we worked on digging a second line of defense trenches and putting up barbed wire, working on roads, and other duties that were part of the engineer's routine. We had to keep the roads open and in shape so that artillery could move over them if necessary to advance.

Lodgement in Belleau Wood was affected by the Marines at great cost but this was not fully taken until about June 25th. During this period, fighting was continuous and bloody in the rough quadrangle formed between Bouresches and Champillon to the south, Belleau and Torcy to the north. Germans and Americans stood there and fought it out. The desperate fighting which won Belleau Wood had all been done by the 5th and 6th Marines, the machine gun battalion, and 2nd Engineers who were constantly with them.

The 7th Infantry entered the sector for a few days, relieving the exhausted Marine Battalion. Their efforts were futile. By June 28, things had become somewhat quiet along the front. The artillery fire was no longer a continuous roll. So, for fear that the enemy might also sleep more or less regularly and lose his fear of the Second Division, it was decided to wake him up again by taking some more of his line from him.

Vaux and Hill 204 were just then giving us the most trouble, so arrangements were made with the French to take Hill 204, and the Second Division was to take Vaux and the line to the northwest. Two battalions were detailed for the work, one from the 9th Infantry to take

Vaux and one from the 23rd to take the line to the north-west of Vaux. Company A of the 2nd Engineers was attached to the battalion from the 9th to help in the attack and consolidate the position. Company C was similarly attached to the battalion from the 23rd Infantry. Company C left its camp at La Croisette Woods on June 30th and joined the battalion from the 23rd Infantry at the jumping-off place. On the evening of July 1st, the infantry went over the top and the engineers waited at the jumping-off place, a ravine, called Suicide Trench. The Engineers then set out and dug them in. The infantry battalion was relieved, and the three platoons of engineers took over the defense of the front line. The 4th platoon of C Company was the reserve.

In the late afternoon of the 1st, in my capacity as runner, I was sent back to the kitchen to show the chow detail the way up to the reserve position. At a crossroad in the wood, I came across a soldier laying on a stretcher, waiting for an ambulance. He grunted a little, so I stopped and asked him if there was anything I could do for him, like a drink of water. He said no but that he would like a cigarette. I lighted one for him, and then he told me that he had seventeen machine gun bullets in his leg and side. All he let out of himself was a mild grunt. On the way back, the chow detail was held up for a half hour due to a heavy bombardment of the wood that we were passing through. Before going back for the chow detail, I had seen bodies brought out of Suicide Trench for burial. Carried in blankets, some were whole, and some in pieces.

Early on the morning of July 2nd, I was sent back with a message to the First Sergeant at Company Headquarters, at the far end of the wood. While there, the Germans started shelling sporadically, one shell out in the clearing, another in the woods, maybe one hundred yards away. If one landed close by, the gas guard would sound the gas alarm, and every few minutes we were putting on our masks.

So a shell came over; I heard the whistle of it and ducked down into a traverse part of the trench system, and just as I got down to the bottom, the shell exploded about three feet from the trench. It took a tree about ten inches in diameter and cleared it right off of the ground. It caved in part of the trench that I had jumped into. I got up and started to shake the dirt out of my face and neck, and the gas alarm had gone on, and I had not heard it. The next thing I knew, I was gagging, trying to breathe. Sergeant Frederic Thompson, our company supply sergeant, held me and directed another one of the young fellows to put my mask on. It took some doing; I fought because I couldn't breathe. Finally, through their efforts, I started to breathe again, painfully. I was directed by the First Sergeant to go to the first aid station which was a matter of 500 to 1000 yards away in another section of the wood. When I got there, three or four fellows were sitting there, a couple I recognized as goldbricks. The medic asked me what my problem was, and I told him.

He said, "Now, I can ticket you and send you to the field hospital, or I can give you some pills that will relieve the hurting. And if they don't relieve it, come back, and we'll send you to the field hospital." Well, after seeing who was waiting to go to the field hospital and not wanting my friends to think that I was yellow, I took the pills, to come back if I didn't get some relief.

While I was gone, George Linglebach, a private and a friend of mine, was sent back with a reply to the message I had brought, and about the time I returned from the first aid station, he came back from Lt. Daniel T. Jerman's position (as in charge of reserves, he was acting company commander). George's face and hands were as red as a beet. He had been badly burned by mustard gas along the trail. He didn't know the real trail as I did, and as a result, he brushed through foliage that mustard gas had settled on during the night. George looked at me as if it was my fault. If I hadn't gone to the first aid station, nothing would have happened to him. Anyway, I went back to my platoon.

Lt. Jerman was inquisitive; he always acted like he had a dislike for me. In some manner, he just always seemed to be picky with me, possibly due to my age or wanting to make a man of me. Shortly after lunch, I was directed to go across the field in front of us which was intersected by the Paris-Metz Highway, and I was told that on the other side of the wood that lay in the distance, maybe a third of a mile away, I would find the 2nd platoon. I went across this open field in plain sight of the enemy, crossed the Paris-Metz road, through another field, and in through the wood. It was just as if I had been there a dozen times before. I found the platoon. Tuffy Smith showed me a German machine gun he had picked up, had running again, pointing at the enemy.[3] We had to wait until relief came, and when the company of the 23rd Infantry filed in to take over, we started out.

As we came to the opening where we could look across to the wood we were to go back through, we saw that it was a mass of smoke and flying branches. The Germans were laying down a terrific bombardment, and I thought to myself, "To go through there, it might injure most of us." So I decided to go down the open road through a small farm village to the crossroad where we had been pinned down the night before when I was bringing up the chow detail.

But before getting there, the Lieutenant whose name I never did know (he was only with us a short time) asked me if this was the way we were supposed to go. "No, sir, I was supposed to take you back through that wood where all the shelling was going on." He did not say any more, but Sergeant Walter Schact and another sergeant came over and, in the course of walking on, patted me on the back and said, "Nice going, kid. That's using your bean." When we got to the crossroad in the wood, I recognized our location. So I took them over to the trail which was out of reach of the bombardment and we went back to kitchens and joined the company. Apparently, the Lieutenant reported to Lt. Jerman who was very displeased with me for not following orders and told me so. He might have dished out some punishment had it not been for Tuffy Smith and Walter Schact coming to my defense and explaining to the Lieutenant the conditions of the heavy shelling and that they thought I had used good judgment. The next day, the company returned to La Croisette Woods and continued work on reserve positions, and rested there.

On July 4, Colonel W.A. Mitchell arrived to relieve Colonel James F. McIndoe of command of the regiment, as Colonel McIndoe had been selected for Corps Engineer of the 4th Corps. Colonel Mitchell was a first honor graduate of West Point and had spent four years there as an instructor. Colonel McIndoe was taken ill suddenly on February 6, 1919, and died at Neuf-Chateau of pneumonia. Thus passed our first regimental commander.

I was called to the company P.C. toward the later part of June, and the Captain put a question to me. He said they had a communication from the Secretary of War, Newton D. Baker, stating that my family had been in communication and stated that I was only sixteen years old and wanted me sent home. The Captain reminded me again that I had taken an oath when I had enlisted, but that didn't bother me any, as other people knew I had taken an oath that wasn't true about my age. He asked me if I wanted to go home and, with all of my friends around there listening, again I didn't want them to think that I was yellow. I said, "No." I wanted to stay. So the matter was forgotten.

During this month of battle, the casualties for Company C amounted to twenty killed, and thirty-eight wounded, of which three were taken prisoner; Arthur Hardy was wounded twice; among four evacuated sick were Lieut. Edward Constantine and Sgt. Charlie Bussle who never returned to us.

As of July 1st, I was promoted to Private 1st Class on the recommendation of Sgt. Ed Waltman. I thought that he did not like me; I guess I was wrong. From July 8th to 10th, the Second Division was relieved by the 26th Division. The 2nd Engineers camped in wood southwest of Montreuil-aux-Lions, refitted, drilled, and did a little work on the Corps defense line until it left on July 16th for its share in the battle at Soissons.

On July 14th, General James Harbord took over and commanded the Division through the Soissons offensive and until July 29th.

Looking back again, for the past month in the early fighting, the men had only their iron rations, and some were without food or water for twenty-four hours due to difficulty of transportation. There was an ammunition shortage in the first hours of the battle. The enemy shelled the whole area heavily. In one brigade area, nearly 22,000 shells fell in twenty-four hours. During the month of continuous fighting that followed, the 2nd Division captured twenty-four officers, 1650 men, and a large number of guns and material.

Because of the bitter nature of the fighting, the division lost heavily, more men than in any other fight. The total casualties were 9,777, of which 1260 were killed on the field and more than 1500 were severely wounded, nearly 7000 slightly wounded, gassed, and missing. At first, hospitals were inadequate for the stream of wounded. In one village, the stretchers were laid out in the open, side by side until nearly an acre was covered by rows of the wounded.

---

1. Jack Fogle is LeRoy G. Fogle, 43rd Co, 5th Marines.
2. The brothers referenced are Glen and Sidney Hill, 79th Company, 6th regiment.
3. I am unable to determine who Tuffy Smith was.

Chapter 5

Chateau Thierry to Soissons

F
or five weeks, the division held the road to Paris; the German drive was halted. Then the 2nd was withdrawn to nurse its grievous wounds.

At this time, Foch was preparing the great counter-offensive that sent the Germans reeling back. The Second was getting replacements to fill up its depleted ranks. On July 16, the division was hastily transported in trucks and unloaded in the Villers-Cotterets region. By night marches through the forest, the division was pushed up to the front. The forest was full of troops moving up to the front line. In the inky darkness and driving rain, the men were forced to march double file, touching one another to avoid being separated.

Reaching the lines only a few minutes before jump-off time, the Second attacked behind tanks at the vital point of the thrust near Soissons. This was the great adventure of the Second Division, the cruelest and most exhausting forced marches it ever made, culminating in a surprise attack so swift and furious that the German lines were pierced to a depth of seven kilometers in as many hours, with enormous loss in men and material.

The 9th and the 23rd Infantry and the 5th Marines led the attack. The 6th, being in Corps reserve, the division reserve, were the 2nd Engineers and the 4th Machin Gun Battalion. The Germans never attacked after July 18, 1918. From that day, they were on the defensive. The Second Division was relieved on July 20th and 21st and proceeded to the Marbache Sector, where it rested during August and where it marched to take part in the first drive of the American Army, against the St. Mihiel salient.

I want to tell about some of Company C's participation at Soissons. On the night of the 18th, C Company found itself on an open sloped area to the east of the town of Vierzy. There on instruction, we dug trenches long enough to hold a squad of men. About fifty yards back of these trenches, we dug our own slit trenches which would hold a squad of men. Early in the morning of the 19th, just about daybreak, the one-man French tanks started across the line, crossing in between the slit trenches, and coming behind them, fifteen paces apart, were the men of our infantry, with their rifles at the ready, joking and kidding as they went along.

On the 18th, the American and French planes had

controlled the air in this sector, shooting down many German planes and losing a few. On the 19th, the Air Force, which was our support on the 18th, moved down to the Chateau Thierry area and around toward Rheims. It seemed like we had started the attack in the area of Soissons, started the enemy back, then they started pushing in from the tip of the salient, the eastern end was the hinge near Rheims. At one time on the 19th, we watched two of our planes, flying low, their numbers were 2 and 10, they would fly out in the direction of the German line and then come hurrying back with many German planes behind them. About ten in the morning, I was asked if I would, in my job as runner, go back and get some water. Many of the men were out of drinking water. So another lad, whose name I have forgotten, and I went back to Vierzy to find drinkable water. I had a stick with fourteen canteens on it. We reached Vierzy safely and snooped around through a couple of factories the Germans had hastily left. We found good water, and then discovered that the first aid station had also been established in Vierzy. There were caves adjoining where farmers had stored grain.

I got back to the company and witnessed eighty some odd enemy planes, at various levels, overhead at the same time, appearing to be in search of the planes of the previous day.

After lunch, I was again asked to go back and get some water which I proceeded to do, accompanied by two other men who had not been back before. One of them was Ted Becker, a friend from another platoon.[1] We hiked into town, filled the canteens, and started back.

Ted Becker had got ahead of us. I was snoopy and wanted to investigate the caves. So the other lad and I went up to see what these caves contained and at that time the Germans started shelling the area with shrapnel and high explosive shells, many of them exploding in front of the first aid station. We started back up to the company and on the way, we ran into Sgt. Richard Mason.

One has to understand that the portion of the terrain about 50 percent of the distance back to the company, and the eastern half of the area from the highway was out in the open, exposed and in view of the enemy. Sgt. Mason appeared pretty well shaken up. He told us that there was no use in our going on because the Germans had got the range on the center line of the trench and had blasted it with shell fire, and those that were not dead or wounded had scattered. Sgt. Mason was shell shocked. He said further that orders were to gather at the kitchens because we were being relieved. We asked him about Ted Becker, who was five minutes ahead of us. His reply was "Ted Becker was in that truck that just went by; he's badly wounded." So we decided to follow his instructions and go to where the kitchens were located.

Unfortunately, I left the canteens behind that I had been carrying, thinking that the owners would have no further use of them, why carry them? Later, I was to pay a penalty for the loss of equipment. When we found the C Co. kitchen we were greeted by Jimmy Higgins and Sgt. Dillon was there, as usual.

As a result of the shelling, covering a period of between thirty minutes and an hour, we lost fourteen men killed. Sgt. Edwin Waltman and Sgt. Alvin Dean were in a shell hole together. Waltman lost both of his legs and Dean lost one. Waltman died there. Dean was evacuated. Our Mess Sergeant Jack Graham was wounded, evacuated, and died in the hospital several days later. A total of fourteen were killed, and one died of wounds. There were thirty wounded, including Captain Samuel Irwin, an officer who had sailed with us, and Lieutenant Arthur Spencer was reported as sick and evacuated.

On July 20th, the regiment was withdrawn from the sector, and it moved by marching to Monthyon near Meaux, arriving there on July 26th, making stops en route. The regiment remained here until July 30th, during which period it took a bath in the Marne River, the first real bath since June 1st. New clothes were received and distributed, and we rested for four days. During these four days, I was confined to company area by Lt. Jerman because I had lost the canteens. Sgt. Louis Vail and Jim Sheridan, who was acting mess sergeant due to the loss of Jack Graham, used me as a runner.

There wasn't much that either one had to do because

most of the company were allowed to go to Meaux and other places unrestrained. The only thing I did in the capacity of runner was to go and buy a bottle of rum at the café in the business section of this small city for the two sergeants. But me, I was being punished by Lt. Jerman, who seemed to take pleasure in it. Finally, Sgt. Vail questioned Lt. Jerman, who was then acting company commander, about my being confined to company area, and his reply was "Oh, I forgot all about that." I was released from any restriction, but it was too late, we moved the next day. I still wonder if he had heard me refer to him as "Dugout Dan."

Looking back at a report of the action at Soissons, the Second and the First American Division along with the First French Moroccan Division, which contained the Foreign Legion, were the spearhead of the fighting on the 18th. We were under the command of the French General Charles Mangin. At Maintz, after the armistice, Mangan said this was the decisive battle of the war. The Second's casualties totaled 3,942 men in the two attacks of the two days. Only 481 were killed on the field. Among the killed, wounded, or gassed were 154 officers. The captured included 66 officers, and 2,899 soldiers, also 75 field guns, and much other booty. The Germans never attacked after this fight. From that time on, they were on the defensive.

The Second Division, which was relieved as I have stated before, proceeded to the Marbache sector where it rested during August, and from which it marched to take part in the first drive of the American Army. During this resting period, we did go back to a front line in the quiet southern end of the front. On July 30, the Second Engineers entrained for its new area. And on July 31, it detrained at Nancy and marched to Champigneulles. Here we were given special engineer drills for five days. My company was then sent to Pont-a-Mousson, which was at one of the kings of the Saint Mihiel salient. On the hike to Pont-a-Mousson, it started to rain, and rain hard. That evening, we fell out in a wood so as not to expose ourselves over a wide area, laid our shelter halves down on the wet ground, and rolled up in our blankets. The next morning, I was lying in a foot of water. The ground was soft and the weight of my body had made a depression in the soil. Of course, by this time, I was a little taller and heavier. I no longer was in the last squad of the fourth platoon which was the tall end of the company. I was in the next-to-last squad. There were some fellows like Stanley Weber, who hadn't grown much. And I had caught up with them; I wasn't as heavy as some of them, I weighed about 130 pounds, and I had gone upward.

We did work on the fortifications at Pont-a-Mousson, strengthening them. I had never before seen such strong defensive trenches, deep dugouts, concrete pillboxes, things made for permanent use. Later, we were stationed along the Marne at Bois-de-l'Eveque. It was a huge army cantonment; it's still in use today from what I note on the French maps. Later we were prepared to go into the Saint Mihiel salient. Pershing had plans to use the Americans in an American Army, not to hand them out piecemeal to the French to use but to have an army of his own to command. So the French hierarchy eventually gave in, and the battle for St. Mihiel was planned and to close the German salient that extended like a bowl down into French land.

After our strenuous fighting at Chateau Thierry and Soissons, the Second Division was badly in need of rest, so General Headquarters decided that this organization should go to the quiet sector, which I have mentioned, and indulge in trench operations until it was ready for another big one. Further along in this record, it will be shown, however, that there was very little resting, and the Second Division was shoved into the fighting again.

---

1. Ted Becker is Theodore Becker.

Chapter 6

St. Mihiel – Blanc Mont – Attigny

On August 15, the Second Division was relieved by the 82nd Division, and four companies of the 2nd Engineers who had been actively engaged in the sector were marched to their new station at Camp Bois-de-l'Eveque near Toul. Company C and F were the last to leave on August 18th. Here we found we were in for work and some training. The work was on a rifle range that the French had failed to complete. The other units of the division used the range after it was completed, and we too had our turn. We had many replacements since Chateau Thierry so training was a continuing function. In the interim, we had other work to do, drilling, working on roads, and various other duties.

General John Pershing insisted that his divisions fight as a unit, as an army instead of being loaned out to bolster the French and the British. He wanted an American sector. He finally got his way.

So on September 1st, the regiment left Bois-de-L'Eveque for its new camp, Bois-de-la-Cumejie. An intermediate stop was made at a town that night, and the following day the regiment resumed its march, arriving at its destination about midnight of the same day. When we were close to the front, all marching and movement of troops had to be done at night to maintain secrecy and avoid any possible observation. We left for Bois-de-Hayes on September 9th, arriving there on the morning of September 10th, my seventeenth birthday. Camp was no sooner established when the order came to be ready to advance. We were getting ready for the attack at St. Mihiel.

The engineers were assigned to various duties; I think there were fifty men from C Co. assigned to go with the infantry as wire cutters. This meant that they would be in the front line of the first wave and would cut the enemy wire for the infantry to pass through. Some men were assigned to go with the tanks; there were one-man Whippet tanks, and an engineer would walk behind them and assist them if they got stuck. Much of the enemy fire would be directed at these tanks. Trestles were prepared if the bridge at Thiacourt was destroyed. Other duties were assigned; most of us worked on the roads, filling in traps or where the Germans had blown out sections of road as deep as 10 feet, to make it impossible for artillery to pass over.

The attack started on the morning of Sept. 12th, and the objective was gained in short order, the city of Thiaucourt. We were only in the fighting for about three days when we were relieved by the 303rd Regiment of Engineers, part of the 78th Division. However, we didn't go very far. We had to return. Something had gone wrong, and they thought we should back up the 78th. However, after another day, things turned out to be OK, so we again turned and left this part of the front.

On September 26, the American assault against the German position in the Argonne Forest began. About that time, General Henri Gourand, the distinguished commander of the 4th French Army, requested the loan of the Second Division in the battle we call the Champagne. We were moved by rail to a point near Chalons-sur-Marne. The region was the most heavily fortified, both by nature of the ground and artifice of war, on the western front, and the Bosche was resolved to hold it at any cost.

The key to the German defense was called Notre Dame de Champs, dominated by Blanc Mont Ridge. I understand that the French had tried three times to break through at this point but failed. Placed under the order of General Gouraud, the Second Division, in an attack delivered on a narrow front from the trenches beyond Souain, broke through to Blanc Mont on October 3rd, seized the ridge and the approaches to it from the north, and held its position in the face of the most stubborn counter attacks it had ever experienced until the French lines to the right and left caught up with us, and the sector was stabilized. With Blanc Mont lost, the Germans retreated out of necessity. Marshall Phillipe Petain called the storming of Blanc Mont Ridge the greatest single achievement of the campaign of 1918, the Battle of Liberation. It was the hardest fighting of the Second Division in casualties and the quality of resistance encountered.

On October 10th, the Second Division was relieved by the 36th Division, their artillery and engineers had not arrived, so the 2nd Artillery Brigade and 2nd Engineers were instructed to join and go forward with the 36th. There were some disastrous things to come.

Nine German Divisions contributed a total of sixty-two officers and 2,234 enlisted men to our bag of prisoners. Besides forty-two pieces of artillery, we captured a vast quantity of other material. The casualties for the 2nd Division totaled 209 officers and 4,766 enlisted men. The majority of these were wounded.

During the early part of October, while the infantry and Marines were fighting to gain their objective, the engineers were occupied with repairing roads. The 4th platoon of C Company was in charge of the engineer dump. This was where the reserve supplies were kept, under Lt. Emil Hohn who built a stockade to hold the German prisoners sent back. Their housing was made from empty ammunition cases piled three high in the center and two high at the outer lower sides. The roofs were of corrugated iron sheets, and bedding in most instances was burlap bags; these items were all that were available. Lt. Hohn had to complete this work of holding the prisoners in a hurry one evening. He was complimented for his efforts, and the prisoners turned over to us were not dissatisfied. The prisoners were utilized in tearing down the remaining stubs of walls of the village of St. Pierre-a-Arnes.

The village, having been in the battle zone for several years, was completely demolished before this battle. The tallest portion of the walls standing were those of the church. It was here that it was brought home to us that the church, one in each village, due to the small steeple and cross, was the tallest building, right in the center of town. The enemy could always use the church as a landmark and determine where to set the sights of his artillery.

The prisoners turned over to us were to be used in breaking up the limestone walls, which was used to fill in shell holes and crater in the roads and highways. We had a group of six to eight prisoners assigned to one or two of us. Of course, our rifles were loaded. We would load trucks to carry the material where needed. The prisoners would line up behind us at meal time and have the same food we had.

They particularly enjoyed our white bread and would line up again just for an extra piece. They had had only schwartzbrot or black bread for a long time. Being able to speak German fairly well, I learned that several of those whom I was guarding were young and close to my age, one of them even a little younger. They were happy that the war was over for them and happy with the way they were treated. So they really applied themselves to the job.

On October 8, the engineers went into the fight again, but this time the entire regiment was used. The French units on the right and left had not kept up with the advance of our troops. Some enemy troops had come in behind ours. On the morning of the 8th, the engineers and the 4th Machine Gun Battalion went into action. Companies A and C under Major John J.F. Steiner went forward to fill the gap in the right of the line, relieving elements of the 9th Infantry and the 36th Division. There was infiltration on the part of the German troops into the area in the rear of the engineers.

I was to learn later that Lt. James Spafford, considered a taskmaster, but liked very much by his men, in cleaning out a machine gun nest was wounded. But he kept on, and he was wounded again and died. On the 8th, I was sent to battalion and regimental headquarters, both of which were located on the top of Blanc Mont in a dugout sixty feet deep on the German side of the slope. On the morning of the 8th, I was detailed to accompany a chaplain and show him the way to the area just south of St. Etienne. Heavy resistance had been encountered at the site of a graveyard. As we approached this area and saw the cemetery, there was a row of our troops, laying and in a few cases kneeling forward against their rifles as if they were in a line of skirmish. The row to the right and left of us looked even and equally spaced, but they were all dead. The Chaplain thanked me, dismissed me with the words that he expected to be there for some time, and that I might be needed at headquarters.

A short time after I returned to Battalion headquarters, Earl Maloney, who was then Sgt. Major, dispatched me to meet a chow detail that was bringing up food for the men in the front line and the other men located at a certain point to assist and direct the detail to each company. From the surface area of this massif, one could look down on all of the wooded breaks and open fields below. The area was of soft limestone, almost chalky. At night, in the moonlight, one could see figures moving about a quarter of a mile away. The soldiers who had dug in, and laid in their dugout, came out all white. We met the detail. C Company's man was one of our newer men, a fine fellow. I wish I remembered his name. He said to me while we were waiting, "Chick, have you any cigarettes? We are all out of smokings. The company got caught in a box barrage: we lost a lot of friends, and I know a smoke will make the fellows up there feel a lot better."

When we left St. Germaine, where we had stopped for a couple of days, I noticed that a lot of fellows threw away or just left sacks of Bull Durham tobacco, which was a bi-weekly or tri-weekly action. I collected 12 sacks of the tobacco and had them in my overcoat pocket. I gave all but one to this friend. He tried to give me all the money he had, but I was embarrassed and refused. I learned later that the tobacco was appreciated by a lot of fellows.

I then returned to Battalion P.C. early on the morning of the 9th. Earl Maloney told me he wanted me to carry a message to Captain Jerman. Yes, he had been promoted. It was just daylight. He pointed down to the opening in the woods below us and called my attention to the soixante track, or narrow-gauge track which is sixty centimeters wide. He said, "Follow that track until you come to an opening to the right a half kilometer from where you start. When you get there, be careful because you will be in plain sight of the enemy. On the other side of the opening is a clearing that is also in sight of the enemy. Straight across that clearing in a northeast direction on that side of the wood, you will find Captain Jerman; give him this message."

I proceeded as instructed. About halfway, walking fast, still not fully awake, I heard "Hey." This really woke me up. It frightened me to a certain degree. A private of the 141st Infantry of the 36th Division was looking for his company. I understood at the time that the enemy had made some kind of counterattack and had scattered a portion of the 141st. This had added to C Company's problem because its men had to take over and cover the area. When I came to the clearing and started across, a bee or bug went by my ear so close that I could hear the buzz, and then another, and suddenly with the third buzz, I realized someone was shooting at me. The fourth one nicked my helmet and made a ping. This was the second time I became really frightened. I don't know if my feet touched the ground for the next thirty or forty feet.

I reached Captain Jerman's point of command, handed him the message, and he looked at me with what I took as a look of wonder that it was me who was delivering the message. I also tried to figure out if his eyes carried just sadness or if he was pretty well shaken up or whether it was fatigue. He told me there was no response so I returned to battalion headquarters. Upon arrival there, I was told to report back to my platoon. There I found that the prisoners had been turned over to the French, and we were to get ready to move up.

On October 12, both battalions were placed on the roads north and south of St. Etienne-a-Arnes for repair and maintenance. The 36th Division was following the retreat of the enemy. That night the regiment camped in and near Machault. On October 14, the work of burying the dead was completed. C Company was stationed near Machault in what appeared to be warehouse buildings of the railroad. The company did work of various types including 60-centimeter railroad repair, bridges, etc. Shortly after being stationed at or near Machault, we received mail for some of the fellows. I had a letter telling me that Jack Fogle was home. Stanley Weber received a letter with the front page of the Long Island newspapers, on the front page a heading "Stanley Weber captures thirty-six Germans single-handed." He, as well as the rest of us, got a bang out of that. At St. Mihiel, Germans were captured who in turn were turned over to us to help in the repair of roads so the artillery and supplies could pass. When finished, two or three of us would take them to the holding area until they could be shipped farther back. Stanley had a group of thirty-six that he took back to the holding stockade. In a letter home, he mentioned this.[1]

A couple of days later, Earl Boyer approached me when neither of us was on a work detail. He wanted to shoot dice with me. I didn't have a lot of money left, maybe twenty or thirty francs which was four or six dollars. He had a small pair of French dice which had rounded corners. I guess he felt this would give him an advantage because those rounded corners would prevent even rolls. Well when we were through bucking heads, I had won about 550 francs from him. This was about 110 dollars in American money. At one time in the session, he ran out of money and asked me to wait. He came back, possibly with borrowed money. That evening, I contacted the YMCA representative and arranged for him to send a money order for $100 to my mother. This was the third time I had made a winning of this size and sent it home. The next day Early wanted a chance to get his money back. I had to inform him that I no longer had the money. He never spoke to me again unless he had to.

About this time, a French soldier came through our area with three German prisoners in his charge, one of them I knew. He had been in my charge in the early part of the month. They were looking in the drain ditches they passed, for what I don't know. This one boy I had taken a liking to; I asked the French soldier if I could talk to them and with his permission I did. The German lad couldn't understand why after being captured by the Americans, why they were turned over to the French. He did not understand that we were on loan to the French Army and would be leaving soon and that we had no facility for keeping prisoners. He told me that they had to work hard, did not get much food, and were not treated as we had treated them. He said the food was terrible. I spoke to Cleon Dawson who was the cook in charge that day. He gave me a loaf of white bread which was of a size of four or five pounds and a can of bacon which weighed about 10 pounds. At first, the Frenchman balked but then said, "OK." I have wondered sometimes if the Germans got to eat it, or did the French take it away from them.

Company C had ten killed and fifteen wounded

during the conflict of Blanc Mont and Attigny. Twenty men were decorated with either a Croix de Guerre or the Distinguished Service Cross or both.

---

1. This article was also published as "Glen Cove Lad Captures 14 Foe," *Brooklyn Times Union*, August 12, 1918, 3.

Chapter 7

The Argonne: Farewell to C Company

At the end of October, the Division concentrated in the Argonne. The artillery brigade and the Second Engineers had not been resting as had the rest of the division, but orders came in calling them away from the 36th Division. It was a tough, two-day hike for us up to the jump-off point. During this hike to the front, after being trucked as close as possible, I remember Frank Keegan. Good old Frank. At that time, he was old enough to be my father, which didn't take a lot of age. Frank, who came from San Francisco, had been in the National Guard before the war. He could not keep up with the hurried marching pace, loaded down as we were. He gradually fell further back as we went along until he was even with me in the next to last squad of the 4th platoon, which was the next to last squad in the company. He looked at me, smiled, and said, "Chick, if you can make it, so can I." And with that, he quickened his step and caught up with his squad in the 3rd platoon. One has to understand that, again, we were carrying our ninety pounds of standard equipment and, in addition, we also carried a large pick or shovel and several bandoliers of ammunition. And we were tired before we started.

On the morning of November 1st, the division jumped off. It attacked the Kremhilde-Stellung line, and of the German strong points, along the line St. Georges, Landres-et-St. Georges, taking over this sector from the 42nd Division. The 2nd broke through and continued to advance, overcoming all resistance through the ten days that followed. The condition facing the 2nd Division was very serious. The previous campaign, from September 26th to November 1st, by the American Army before the 2nd Division joined it, had shown that the Germans realized the desperate situation in which they were placed. The Americans were almost within reach of their railroad through Monday and they knew that if the Americans broke this railroad, they would be utterly unable to supply their troops by their single remaining line of supply through Leige, north of the forest of Ardennes. It was then a final struggle between the best German divisions and the American army. The Second Division, with the 89th on its right and the 80th on its left, was ordered to go over the top on November 1st and break the last line of the German defense. All possible artillery was brought up; the barrage was probably the most intense of the war. We had the First Division and the 42nd Division artillery in addition to our own.

From September 26 to November 1, the commanding general had been worried by the road almost as much as by the Germans. In fact, from October 15th to November 1st, it had been reported necessary to stop the advance partly because of the condition of the roads. It was raining more or less continually and the roads were getting worse and worse. Consequently, practically all of the engineers were to be used on the roads and the 2nd Engineers looked forward to hard, grueling, wearisome days of road maintenance, without any of the excitement of battle. The bridges over the river at Landres-et-St. Georges were particularly critical points in the roads, and Colonel Mitchell ordered the engineers to get right on the heels of the infantry and to repair or rebuild these bridges no matter how heavy the enemy's fire. The special details for wire cutters, trap hunting, and artillery assistance were rendered as usual. Company A supplied 25 men as wire cutters; Company B, 55 men as wire cutters; Company C, 22 men were detailed to the tanks, 50 trap hunters; Company D, 25 men as wire cutters, 200 for artillery details; Company E, 50 men as wire cutters, 40 men at engineer dumps, the rest for road work; Company F, all for road work.

The regiment was considerably short of personnel, owing to sickness and lack of replacements. The men on the road work details encamped in a ravine about two miles south of Landres-et-St. Georges, ready to proceed to that town and repair bridges so that there could be no possible delay. Colonel Mitchell realized the situation was very serious and that the Regiment, having been in the front of battle for a month without rest, needed every possible encouragement.

Consequently, on the afternoon of October 31, he assembled all the officers and called their attention to the seriousness of the situation. They were told to seize every opportunity to rest the men, that under no circumstances were the men to be allowed to sleep on the ground if a house could be possibly be secured, that no men would endeavor to seem busy purely for the effect on a general or another staff officer who came by, that every man would be forced to work hard when he worked and would be allowed to lie down and rest when he rested. It seems pertinent to remark here that the Regiment kept up its record for work in the next ten days. The battle started, and we started. The men on the road work followed the infantry promptly into Landres-et-St. Georges, losing twenty men on the way and later in the town. They found that the bridges had not been destroyed, also that the bridges in St. Georges, the next town to the west, had not been broken.

Consequently, the road work was lighter than expected. Special details were sent temporarily to assist in repairing the roads for the dressing station as the ambu-

lances were finding great difficulty in approaching the
station and there was considerable delay. During the
second and third days, the 2nd and 3rd of November, we
worked on roads, filling in tank traps. Another lad and I
had been left at one of the traps to put the finishing
touches on it, with instructions to catch up with the
platoon when it was completed. Finishing our chore, as we
approached a very small village we noted a dead German
officer laying close to the road. We stopped, looked him
over, and debated whether we should take the beautiful
shammy skin vest that he was wearing. As we decided not
to, we heard a footstep, turned and saw an officer coming
close to us. We stood at attention. However, he said, "At
ease, up here we won't stick to formalities. That is a good-
looking vest isn't it? However, like you, I would hesitate to
take it off a dead man." He smiled at us, waved his hand,
and went on. We realized that this officer was General
John A. Lejeune, Commander of the Division. Walking
alone behind the advance. He certainly was a wonderful
commander, officer, and gentleman.

I can remember after leaving Landres-et-St. Georges,
and as we got out into what had been no-mans-land, the
road cut through a small hill, and in the banks alongside
the road were men of the 165th Infantry, the famous
"Fighting 69th of New York" part of the 42nd Division.
There were several lying in the ditch on each side of the
road. They had dug into the embankment and had been

caught out in no-mans-land by some German counterattack. The company had to fall back, and they had to dig in where they were. They were all dead, some of their faces gone, a couple with the tops of their head missing. It was a gruesome sight.

I had not felt good for some time, and on the night of November 3rd, the company was stationed in Bayonville, a walled town. I stopped off at the first aid station and the doctor, after examining me, put a ticket on my blouse and said, "You're on your way to the hospital." I had been running quite a temperature. Another lad from my platoon was there, a newer man whose name I have forgotten; I didn't know him very well. I asked him if he would tell the first sergeant and my squad corporal that I had been sent to the hospital. He said he would. He forgot because after I returned home, I found out that I was reported missing in action.

On the night of the third, we who were to go to the hospital were loaded into a hospital train which pulled out on the morning of the fourth, for Base Hospital 68 and other hospitals in the area of Nevers which is in the center of France. Close to a week later, there was a lot of music, bands playing, automobiles sounding their horns, cheering, hollering, and singing going on outside in the roadways of the hospital, and somebody said, "The armistice is going to be signed tomorrow at 11 o'clock." This did not awaken anything in me; the armistice didn't mean anything. The only thing I was interested in was the end of everything. The next day, after the armistice was signed, I realized why they were making so merry because the armistice had been signed and the conflict stopped.

A couple of days later, a wounded man was put in the bed next to mine, and he asked me what outfit I was out of. I told him and he responded with, "Oh, you know, that outfit of yours in something. We crossed over one of the bridges that they built over the Meuse River. When we got there you could look both ways and there was nothing but dead men laying around, dead engineers. They really went through something." I found out later that two companies of the engineers had laid two-foot bridges across the Meuse, assisted by two companies of the 9th Infantry. All of the companies involved suffered heavy casualties. The enemy was located on the heights above the river on the east side, and though it was known that the armistice was to be signed on the next morning, the fight carried on until that hour.

The following message was written by General John A. Lejeune, Division Commander:

France, November 12, 1918.

On the night of November 10, heroic deeds were done by heroic men. In the face of heavy artillery and withering machine gun fire, the Second Engineers threw two-foot bridges across the Meuse, and the first

and second battalions of the 5th Marines crossed reso-
lutely and unflinchingly to the east bank and carried
out their mission. In the last battle of the war, as in all
others in which this division has participated, it
enforced its will on the enemy.

John A. Lejeune, Major General
U.S. Marine Corps, Commanding

Going to the hospital terminated my affiliation with C
Company and with the Second Engineers. I was in Base
Hospital 68 for about a month and a half and then was
moved to Base 123, a convalescent hospital. Both were
located in the center of France near Nevers.

In the middle of February, we were informed that we
could not return to our regiments in the Army of Occupation, because they had been filled by replacements, so we
were sent to the 86th Division to go home. This division
had come over a short time previously and had been used
for replacement purposes. After about a week of what
appeared to be mistreatment on the part of these shavetails
called officers, or the lack of knowledge that they were
dealing with men who had gone through a lot of warfare,
all had been injured in some way, while they would never
have that experience, an officer from General Headquarters came through looking for volunteers. He told us that
they were forming six battalions of Military Police to do
duty in the Army of Occupation, not with our soldiers but

with the civilian population. It took him three days to raise the 1200 men that he wanted, out of the 1800 that had come from the hospital.

After a few days, we were shipped to the headquarters of the Military Police, and we went into training. We were sent shortly to do duty with American soldiers. This was to be of short duration and part of a brief training. There were four or five of us to a village, and in the course of this training, in one village, five of us were stationed with one of the companies of the famous Lost Battalion. We made many friends as we went.

Soldiers were not allowed to have anything heavier than light wines or beer, but we would tell them that if they would get into a back room, and be quiet, not to make any noise that would cause some officer to want to investigate, fine, we wouldn't say anything; we would allow them to stay until 10 o'clock. Orders were that the cafés had to close at nine. The last unit that we were assigned to was a black one. All of the enlisted men were black; all of the officers were white. They were very restricted; they weren't allowed much of anything. We came into town, and the lad I had become buddies with, Dick Chandler from Atlanta, Georgia, who had served with the Third Division, and I were wandering out toward the end of the town. We had seen several blacks walking out that way so we became curious. And lo and behold, we found a room full of enlisted men in a building, a café, way out at the far end of the village. And they were really whooping it up.

Dick and I went in, and you could hear a pin drop. We were spoiling their fun. Anyway, we had a talk with them, and we said, "Now look fellows, if you'll be quiet, you know what your instructions are, we don't want you to get in trouble with your officers. If you want to come out here, and you want to play it cool, and be quiet, and break it up by nine or ten o'clock, fine, we'll come out and have a drink, too, sometimes." Well, at this, many cheers sounded, and, for the short time we were with this unit, before their leaving for the United States, we had made many friends.

When we were shipped to Germany, we were sent to an area between the Rhine and the Moselle, up in the hilly country. We were assigned horses, taught to ride, and patrolled various sections, making two-day trips, resting the third day at headquarters, and drilling on horseback.

The next assignment of the 281st M.P. Co. was a move to Coblenz, Germany, where we were assigned the bridge-heads, the railway stations, and the city prison. We were no longer mounted. There wasn't anything spectacular about this work, or difficult. We did not have duty with any troops of our own except those in the city prison and were on their way to Leavenworth, to serve five to twenty years.

I got word of where the Second Engineers and particularly C Company were stationed, north of Coblenz in a small city by the name of Engers, located on the east side of the Rhine River. I was able to get up there on three occasions during the next couple of months. Before my first visit, I had been informed that, if a formal written request was made by the company commander, I could be transferred back to C Company. When I explained this to Jim, he took me to see Lieut. George Knight who at that time was acting Company Commander. Lieut. Knight told me that he would be very happy to do this. I would then be able to return home with my friends.

Captain Jerman was on an assignment at battalion headquarters, and when visiting the company on the second occasion a couple of weeks later, I was informed by Anthony Koldoff, who was company clerk, that Jerman had killed the request. He also had, on the basis that I was reported as missing in action on Nov. 3rd, killed two recommendations for decoration, made by sergeants who were aware of the incidents related to my actions as a runner on July 1st and 2nd. That I had been injured and had continued to do my duties. That on October 8th, three months later, I still performed my duties, under terrific shell and sniper fire. I think I know why he disliked me, but I could be wrong. He too was not decorated.

Jimmy always seemed happy to see me. Many of the old timers were gone. Tom McCormick wasn't there; he was away, teaching people something in athletics. On the third occasion that I visited Engers, Jimmy took me over to the railway yard and showed me the box car with the kitchen set up in it. They were leaving in two days for home. I felt bad; I would have liked to have been able to go with them. I said goodbye to all of my friends; I failed to get addresses. In fact, I didn't think of it; I thought it would be easy to find them.

About a week later, our new company commander of the 281st, at the first inspection of his new command, was going up and down the lines asking questions. I noticed most everyone was nodding their heads yes. When he came to me he said, "Do you like the Military Police?" And I said "No." And his response to that was, "Why?" I told him I wanted to go home. There were twenty of us out of a little over two-hundred who had nerve enough to respond this way. We had got wind that we were to be sent to other parts of Germany, and I did not want to go. So there were twenty of us who, about a week later, were shipped out as casuals.

On the way from Coblenz, we stopped at Toul, changed trains, and boarded the Paris Express. When we got to Paris, we had to change again for a train to go to Brest, where we would board a ship for that part of our journey home. There was a corporal in charge of us who had all of the travel orders. One of the young lads who was with us disregarded the corporal's warning about getting back on time. He wanted to go and see a girl that he had met in Paris. As a result, we left Paris without him. None of the rest of us had this desire. We had not been to Paris previously and had no desire to risk missing that train. The only consequence of this lad's late return was that he would be picked up by the MPs of Paris, who were noted as a tough bunch, and land in the Paris jail of the American Military Police.

We proceeded on to Brest. I found that the last of the 2nd Engineers, the first battalion, had just sailed. We were there about a week when we were assigned to leave on the USS *Grant*, a former German freighter, converted to one of our navy supply ships, and again converted to a troop transport. I know that the Second Division paraded up Broadway in New York City to much cheering and were accorded a hero's welcome home, which they deserved. The nineteen of us who came back to the U.S. on the USS *Grant*, all veterans of combat units, came home quietly, without any fanfare. We did get a few waves from people traveling on the ferry boats in New York harbor. We landed and were sent to Camp Dix where we went through examinations to make sure that we were not coming home diseased, or lousy. We were given new clothes and then sent to other termination points closer to our homes. I was sent to Camp Grant, Illinois. That was the closest to the home that I was going to. I was discharged and arrived home on August 26, 1919. I had been in the service for two years and four months and had been overseas for two weeks less than two years.

Looking back at this time, and thinking of the men I

had served with, there were twenty-one of them who were decorated with the Croix de Guerre; two of them received two of them. There were seven Distinguished Service Crosses, and in three cases they were to men who also received the Croix de Guerre. And in looking at the casualties of the regiment, five officers were killed in action, four died of wounds, twenty-six officers were wounded, and the major casualties of the regiment including the officers was 219 men killed and 871 men wounded or gassed, for a total of 1,090 men of the regiment. The Second Division suffered the greatest losses of any American Division in the war. Killed in action and died of wounds totaled 5,137; there were 17,138 wounded in action. So the total battle casualties for the division was 23,217.

The entire Division was awarded the Fourragere by the French. The only Division as a whole to receive this honor. The 2nd was the only Engineer regiment to be so honored during World War I.

"Ardor and Tenacity," the motto of the 2nd Engineers was taken verbatim from the citation of the French Army for the extraordinary effort of the Engineers in the battle of Soissons.

Chapter 8

Hail and Farewell to Old Friends

L et me go back to 1919. After I had returned home to my family in Chicago, I found that with the report that I was missing in action, and although the $15.00 was deducted from my pay each month, my allotment to my mother had not been sent to her during the last 11 months of service. This was corrected with the aid of the Red Cross. Several of my old schoolmates tried to entertain me, and while visiting Willis Whipple, his older brother, Dick Whipple, who had been in the service, made me aware of the new organization, the American Legion. I became a charter member of North Shore Post, Chicago. A couple of weeks later, he questioned me about my cough and suggested that I go to the office of the organization handling medical problems for the veterans. So I did. The doctor who examined me in October of 1919, recommended that if I could do so, he would suggest that I got to the west side of the Rocky Mountains, I was rated about 20 percent disabled with chronic bronchitis.

Also during the middle of October, as I was walking south on La Salle Street, who should I run into but Bill Lander. He and his brother had a show, Lander Brothers, that was playing at the Star and Garter which at that time was a burlesque theater, Bill had a theatrical background. He was in one of the company quartets while in the service. Bill insisted that I accompany him to the theatre where he introduced me to his brother and all of the cast. I felt a little uncomfortable around all those half-dressed chorus girls so after a bit, I excused myself and left with the promise that I would come back and go to lunch. I have forgotten why, but I could not make it.

I was sick off and on all winter and spring. Had what I thought was the "flu" three times. In the spring of 1920 at a temporary Veterans Hospital on the south side of Chicago, I again was advised that I would be better off on the west side of the Rocky Mountains, in the southwest so in June of 1920, I started west.

That spring had been a tough one. On Easter Sunday of 1920, a blizzard blew in Chicago, snow drifted up as far as the front doors on the porches, and it was cold. This was what finally decided me to get to a milder climate. I called my brother Nick and told him that I was leaving and why. I asked him to contact my mother and tell her. It was terribly hard to tell people that I very seldom felt good and convince them because I was not sure what was wrong with me. All I knew was the diagnosis, Chronic Bronchitis, a 20 percent or so disability allowance, and a check each month for $28.00.

Bill Wahler, a former classmate, and a real friend, and I went to night school for two semesters. This did help in years to come. Bill and I generally got together on Sundays. We would go to church together, and in the afternoon, we would go to a theatre and see one of the latest films and the accompanying stage show. In the evening there usually was a penny ante poker game at the Wahler flat, and on some occasions, I participated.

During this period of being in Bill's company, we had conversations relative to Jack Fogle, and on occasions about John Dewey Flannigan, another classmate. There were three of us who were from the same class, all under the age, of fifteen or sixteen, Jack had been in the Marine Corps, and Dewey had enlisted in the Navy at sister with the consent of his parents. Dewey, as we called him, was on the Navy Collier, the *Cyclops*, which disappeared while passing through the Bermuda Triangle. Not a trace of the ship was ever found. Bill told me that he had spent a lot of time with Jack Fogle, who had left for Missoula, Montana before I came home. Bill died of pneumonia when he was twenty-five.

I left Chicago in June and went to Mitchell, South Dakota, where I worked in the harvest fields for a while. This work was too dusty. I went from there to Denver once again. I worked on the street cars for a couple of months, with plenty of good fresh air and no strenuous labor. The short period in the harvest field had done me no good. I left Denver before winter set in.

I eventually wound up in Los Angeles, where in 1922, while driving through the downtown area, I saw a fellow walking that I recognized. I stopped the little panel truck I was driving and called to him. He came over to the truck and I asked, "Aren't you Leonard Hillstead?" He said, "Yes." And then, "By God, you are Chick Hubert." He got into the truck, and I took him to his transportation. Here started a renewal of friendship that still prevails.

In 1924, I was working as a quarantine guard for the County during a hoof and mouth disease epidemic. I was stationed at an entrance to the Santa Ynez Ranch, off of Santa Monica Canyon. I had to hike to Pacific Palisades one morning. A tractor pulling a truck caught up with me, and the driver asked me if I would like a ride as he was going to Pacific Palisades too, which at that time was in the early stages of development. A few seconds after the vehicle got underway, I looked at the driver a little closer, and smiling said to him, "Were you a member of C Co., 2nd Engineers during the last war?" "Is your name Hendrix?" He stopped the tractor, looked at me, and said "Yes, by God, that's my name. Who the hell are you?" When I told him, he looked at me closer, grabbed me, and said, "Chick, am I glad to see you. You know, you are the first one I have seen from the old bunch." Shortly after that Tex, Leonard, and I got together.[1] The three of us would see each other at monthly meetings of the Los Angeles Branch of the 2nd Division Association.

In 1924, Leonard told me of meeting Dan Nugent. Dan was a sergeant and well-liked. We got together a few times, and he told me that Jim Casburn had stayed in the service and was 1st Sergeant of C Co. Shortly after that, Dan left Los Angeles for the Mother Lode country. I was told that he was raising frogs. I never heard from him again.

The 2nd Engineers were in Texas. I wrote to Jim and as a result, he and I corresponded for a number of years, in the course of which he informed me of the award of the Fourragere. He sent me a silk one, also a copy of the History of the 2nd Engineers, AEF, 1916-1919. Later and during World War II, Jim worked up to the rank of Major. After World War II, I lost track of him. I understand that he died shortly thereafter.

Also during 1924, Dr. E. Moffitt, who had been keeping tabs on me, insisted that I have some lab work done. As a result, it was found that there was some activity in one of my lungs. Knowing that I had been having negative results with the Veteran's Bureau, I went back again, and again they could find nothing. So he took the job of helping me cure myself. He caused me to become acquainted with the Reniger family. I went to work for them, first as a chauffeur, and later I became Mr. Reniger's assistant. I was treated more like a member of the family. I traveled across the country with him and became acquainted with many prominent people. I was a good listener and digested many things that helped me further my education. The market crash of 1929 caught up with Mr. Reniger in 1930. As a result, upon our return to Los Angeles from New York, my job with him ended. But not our friendship.

In early 1930, while in New York, I passed the Orpheum Theater. Listed on the marquee it read, "The

Lander Brothers." Sure enough, I had another great visit with Bill, happy smiling Bill. He told me where to find Arthur Chaplin in New Jersey and urged me to take the time for a visit with Chappie, as we called him. Lander and Chaplin had been smart in the service. They both went through the preliminaries and became cooks. They were part of the company quartet and worked with Jim Higgins and sang with him. I drove over to Jersey and had a very happy meeting with Chappie. He told me that Checkley was at home and working for the city of Paterson. Bill had returned from a prisoner of war camp in Germany with a withered arm. Chappie begged me not to try to see him for fear that the excitement of meeting me again might cause him to do something that would result in his losing his job.

Arriving back in Los Angeles around June 1st, I found that the Los Angeles Branch of the 2nd Division Association was preparing to host the 10th National Reunion of the Association. Leonard Hillstead was president that year of the Los Angeles Branch and put on the finest reunion that I ever attended. His wife, Florence, was active in the Auxiliary. I guess it was Leonard who told reporters about me, because on the front page of the *Evening Herald* of June 6th was a picture and a short description. George Green showed up for the luncheon, and Carl Gustafson and his wife Babe drove down from Eureka, 900 miles away. Carl, Leonard, Tex Hendrix, and I had a ball.

In the meantime, I had cured myself of my lung trouble. In 1929, after the depression set in, I visited the Chicago area for five months. Bill Becker, one of my school days friends, had me to his home on many occasions. I met quite a few of his friends, and two of his wife's sisters, Esther and Christine. Again in the summer of 1931, on my way back to California, I stopped off in the Chicago area and stayed for a while. I stopped off at the home of my mother and brother Anthony in Waukegan, Illinois. My older brother, Nicholas, was in business there and he offered me a short time job. When the work was finished, he had me go to his company doctor, who in examining me found things the Government doctors had failed to find and confirmed Doctor Moffett's diagnosis of the early 1920s.

Dr. Brannion gave me a note of referral to the Service Officer of the Homer Derringer Post of Waukegan. It explained his findings: scars on the lower right lung. I was then referred to the Legion service officer at Edward Hines Hospital, Maywood, Illinois. While there, I became a member of the Homer Derringer Post. As a result of the efforts and knowledge of the Legion representatives, a compromise was reached, I was given a Statutory Award on the basis that the private evidence was stronger than that of the Veterans Bureau. Thanks to their efforts on my behalf, I felt indebted to the Legion.

In 1933, the 2nd Division Association had its reunion in Chicago, during the Century of Progress exhibition.

Here was something else again. I ran into Ralph Lundgren, Henry Matthews, Earl Maloney, Everett Miller, and Colonel Mitchell. Henry had attained the rank of Regimental Supply Sgt. and Earl that of Regimental Sgt. Major. Ralph and I kept in contact through correspondence. He became president of the Association a few years later and then as chairman of the Division Monument committee, was responsible for the construction and placement of the 2nd Division monument in Washington D.C.

Esther and I were married in Chicago in March of 1934, in fact on St. Patrick's Day. I assisted in organizing the Wells Park Post in Chicago, transferring from the Waukegan Post. Shortly after this, in September of that year, I talked her into quitting her job and going to California with me. Henry Matthews and his wife Evelyn had us to lunch at the Palmer House, a farewell token before we left. I learned that Bill Lander had died in New York, and a few years later I learned that Chappie too had left us. These men died before they were fifty. A little bit too early.

Carl Gustafson had told me where to look for Charlie Brunner, so on a trip to the San Francisco area, Charlie and I got together; he insisted that I spend the night with him and his mother at their home in Richmond, which I did. Charlie was an engineer with the Standard Oil Co. of California. After that, every four or five years, we would see each other, and in between the time, we kept in touch by writing. Through the years, off and on, I heard from many old comrades. Tex Hendrix died a year after World War II, still a young man. I have to smile every time I think about this loving, joking, smiling guy. I have a feeling that almost all of us who were not major casualties during the fighting came home with something wrong with us due to gas or conditions existing during the battle periods.

In 1935, Leonard Hillstead encouraged me to transfer into the American Legion Post that he had been Commander of—Blue Devils of America Post #368. The members were all in combat units, and the name was taken from the term the Germans used for the French Alpine troops who wore a dark blue uniform, France's best fighters. I found that the membership of the Post was small by choice, and composed mainly of veterans of the combat divisions. I became very active in the work of the Post. In 1939, I was elected Historian, and in 1940, 2nd Vice Commander. Elected 1st Vice Commander in 1941, and in 1942, shortly after the start of World War II, I was elected Commander. After finishing my job as Commander, I was named Chairman of the Americanism Committee, a position I held for five years.

My organization work with the Legion helped me in the following years in advancement to higher positions in the Postal Service. Blue Devils Post, shortly after World War II had to move to new quarters, a less desirable place. With the death of many old timers, and others moving to other parts of the State and Country, the ranks thinned and with the lack of recruitment of eligible men from World War II, attendance fell off to the point of a lack of a quorum, so in the middle 1960's the Post disbanded. I transferred to Hollywood Post #43, where I retained my membership after moving to San Diego.

I retired from Government Service at the end of 1964. In 1967, Esther and I moved to San Diego. Anthony Koldoff and his wife visited us here and we, in turn, visited with them in Phoenix. In 1968, seven of us got together during a West Coast reunion in San Diego. Carl and Babe came down from Eureka, Charlie and Jewel, Joe Fazio and his wife, and Lloyd Anson, all from the Bay area, Hillstead came down from Los Angeles and he and Anson were guests of Byron Skelton who lived in San Diego at that time. Tony was too sick to come.

We all enjoyed this get-together. I also received responses that shocked me, telling me of the passing of an old friend, Lundgren, Eben Higby, Emory Warnock, and while we were having a good time, Henry Matthews left us. Since 1968, others have thinned our ranks, with the passing of Jess Lloyd, Tom Golden, Earl Maloney, Brunner, Fazio, Carl Gustafson, Cleon Dawson, Ted Becker, and Bill Sheets.

As near as I can determine there are only eight of us left. All of my old schoolmate friends are gone, Jack Fogle and Bill Becker passed just before their 76th year. I am feeling a little lonesome. I have my family and one personal friend of long-standing, Russell Bryant, but he is more than a thousand miles away. We keep in touch, but he is the only one.

Two old-time friends in the service also acted like older brothers to me. David Jones and Tom McCormick. I never did locate David. Three years ago Jim Higgins sent me Tom's address. During visits to Chicago, in later years, I had unknowingly passed within two blocks of his home several times. He appeared in his response to my letter, just as happy to hear from me as I was to hear from him. We made plans for a get-together with Jim in July of 1978, during the reunion in Chicago.

However, after a trip to Seattle in May, a sleeping bug woke up in my bronchials for some reason. With the help of one of my good doctors, we got rid of it by the end of summer. I had to postpone plans until June of 1979. We again looked forward to this time. A week before Christmas of 1978, I received word Tom had died due to a heart attack. He was eighty-seven. The end of a dream of sixty years, a get-together with a brother-like friend. I don't recall having shed tears before in my adult life, but I guess as one gets old, one is more prone to tears. Jim, at eighty-six, said he was still anticipating my visit.

The spring of 1979 is now in the past, and our pilgrimage back to Illinois and Indiana is a pleasant memory. In June, Esther and I drove from the Chicago area to Dyer, Indiana, to see Jim Higgins, and though Edith, his wife, is in a nursing home, he arranged to give us all of one afternoon. We spent several hours with Jim and his daughter and enjoyed every moment. Jim wanted us to come back for dinner some evening. However, the distance was too great to drive again, our time being limited. Just before saying goodbye for the last time, Jim said, "Chick, in the '20s, I have forgotten if it was in the early or middle 20s, I received a telephone call. The fellow at the other end of the line asked me if, while I was in the service, did I ever know of a fellow in my outfit that threw nine straight naturals. I told him that the only one that I ever knew of that did this was Chick Hubert, and the fellow hung up. I don't know yet who made the call." Strange that all of my old friends should remember my skill when I have tried to forget it, by not indulging.

---

1. Tex Hendrix is James F. Hendrix.

1971 - Going Back

During the late summer and early fall of 1971, Esther and I made a trip to Europe. We joined a tour in London and flew to Amsterdam on my 70th birthday. And after a three-week trip through several countries, we ended the tour in Paris. And now I was to fulfill a dream of fifty years, a personal trip to places of interest to me, back to Memories. Unfortunately, while on the tour, Esther picked up a flu bug that went through the bus, so she was not up to par.

Reservations were made by a representative of the AAA for the train and the hotel in Nancy. Nancy is the capital of the province of Lorraine, and the hotel, the Gran Palace, situated next to the opera house, had originally been the palace of the Duke of Lorraine. The hotel, City Hall, the opera, and other buildings were built facing Stanislaus Square. The room reserved for us had been the room Marie Antoinette had used when she visited the

Duke. However, we decided that it was too elaborate, so we took one less pretentious.

On the second day, after renting a car, we drove to Colombey-les-Belles where I showed Esther the first billet, a hay loft, that I had slept in and pointed out our evening headquarters, the café at the head of the street. We did not utilize cafés every evening, but once or twice a week. Colombey was about twenty-four kilometers south of Nancy, and now on the main highway that leads to Neuf-Chateau. From Colombey we drove to Bairsey-au-Plain, the second small village we were billeted in. Here I noticed that the fountain and trough in the center of the village where people had got their water and on occasion some women washed their clothes, was dry and rusty. Small villages now appeared to have water to the homes as there was a large water tank on a platform located near the center of the village and also located higher than the roofs of the farm houses.

I also noticed that, among these two-story structures, one or two were painted in bright colors. The remainder appeared to look the same, a dull off-white, as we had left them in 1917. I don't imagine any of the latter had been painted. Also, two other things were called to mind.

In a couple of cases, instead of being utilized as the hay loft, the second floors were now converted for residential use and there were no manure piles in front of each house. They had disappeared. In front of a few of them, flowers were blooming or a lawn had been planted. The population of these villages was a matter of two or three hundred, sometimes fewer.

We drove on to Sanzey, passing through the outskirts of Toul. We had been stationed close to Toul on several occasions. I wanted to show Esther the wall around the city, its gates from olden times, and the beautiful cathedral, but we had to change our plans. On the third day, we left Nancy and drove to Chateau Thierry. We were there for several days. On one day, we visited the huge monument built by the American Battle Monument Commission to commemorate the battles that took place in the Chateau Thierry area and at Soissons. It is located on Hill 204, which was a tough one to take. The French name is "Cote 204." The story and the shoulder patch of the divisions who fought in the area are on the monument. It is dedicated to both the Americans and the French.

On the second day, we drove to Lucy-le-Bocage, where we saw the first of the boulders located in most of the villages in that area, they bear the insignia of the Second Division, the Star and Indian Head. Then we drove through Belleau Wood. We stopped to take a picture of the bronze stele in the center of the road. It has a figure of a charging Marine on it. The road is in the form of a circle at this point with various types of ordnance, machine guns, 75s, mortars, and other equipment stationed around the perimeter of the circle. The wood was renamed by the French to honor the Marine Brigade and it was named Bois de la Brigade de Marine. Then we drove on to the cemetery at the east end of the wood.

The cemetery has thirteen curving rows on each side of the flagpoles which line the center walk, a row for each stripe in the flag. In the first row, the fifth grave, I found Orra L. Snyder. Then in the third row, eighty-third grave, I found Jack Graham, mess sergeant. He died four days after being wounded at Soissons on July 19th. I stopped looking at graves and went into the chapel. Here I got a shock. There were 1,080 names carved into the walls, names of soldiers who were missing in action. 250 lay in graves marked "Unknown," and 830 were never found, most of whom fought with the Second, in or near Belleau Woods or with the First and Second at Soissons. Among the names on the wall were those of Corporal Frank Lillis and my friend Sgt. Edwin D. Waltman.

This left me with a deep feeling of grief, and humility, to think there I was reading names of friends who had died fifty-three years previous, out there somewhere, lost, never found. It made me appreciate that Someone must have been looking out for me. It brought back to mind that, early in June when we were digging graves, I had been asked to go after water to drink. And again, on July 19th at Soissons, I had been detailed to show a couple of other fellows where to fill canteens with drinking water, and while we were gone enemy shells were again the cause of deaths, many, and Ed. Waltman was among them.

I was saddened to the point that I wanted to wait for another day to go back. As I was walking away from the chapel, I did go back for another look at the graves of Snyder and Graham. As I strolled along the third row, I came to the grave of Cpl. George Bell, killed on the 6th of June, and that of Jim Highly, reported as wounded and missing. But he died on the 7th of June.

The Superintendent of the cemetery, Arthur Darios, was most kind and courteous. He allowed me to check the register covering the burials in all of the cemeteries, furnished me with pamphlets, and a few out-of-print post-cards, and told me where to get further information. When I left, I returned to Snyder's grave once more.

Others that I had looked for apparently had been shipped home. I looked at all of the graves from a distance: a gentle breeze of October was blowing. If I can call a cemetery beautiful, this one is. The grass is very green, and the plants and trees afford a beautiful landscape, well-kept and fittingly taken care of. The men who died and rest here are better-taken care of than in many cemeteries in our country. If only it was closer to home. Visitors are few these days, and though it is beautifully cared for, I feel that it is very lonely.

When I look back on this visit, I think of all the fine fellows we left behind. I also think of all of those that I have had the pleasure of seeing or writing to. It is my firm belief that most of the fellows who went through the Chateau Thierry and Soissons portion of the fighting and lived, even though they were not wounded, had some physical deterioration due to inhaling poison gas without being aware of it or having to exist for weeks at a time in a hole in the ground, dry or wet. Some of these died in the late twenties, in the thirties, and so on. I have been shocked many times by letters, written by widows, or a member of a good friend's family, telling me how they had suffered before they died. I still have most of those letters.

In early 1942, when the convoys would roll down Hollywood and Sunset Boulevards, heading for the railroad or for a ship in the harbor, I would feel the urge to shout, "Hey, wait for me!" But I would realize that it was futile thinking on my part. I was too old, disabled, and had a family that I could not leave. Yet whenever I see that poster of Uncle Sam, I feel that finger is pointing at me.

Going back once more; I remember our association with the Marine Brigade. The highest compliment that they ever extended was, "They are almost as good as we are." This applied to us. In July of 1974, the 53rd reunion of the 2nd Division association was held in San Diego. Lieutenant General Merwin Silverthorn, USMC, retired, was the speaker at the banquet. He reminisced on the rough going during the battles for Belleau Wood and at Soissons, and in his concluding remarks, said, "Let us not forget our friends, the Engineers; without them we may not have made it." General Silverthorn was commissioned on June 9th, 1918, so went into the latter part of the battle for Belleau Wood, and at Soissons, as a platoon commander. In a recent correspondence he stated, "Indeed, the Marines' respect and admiration for the 2nd Engineers knew no bounds."

Ephram Testerman, now living in San Diego, attended his first reunion, and also appreciated the comments of General Silverthorn. Ephram was wounded during the battle for Attigny, he returned to the Company when it was stationed on the Rhine.

In the spring of 1978, while on a vacation, the letter carrier left a package with a neighbor. When I opened it, I found the Purple Heart, also the accompanying citation. Sent to me sixty years after having inhaled that does of gas, in recognition that I had been wounded and had continued to do my duty. When I look at this medal, hanging on the wall, in a case with other incidental decorations, it brings back all of the happy, sad, and frightening memories. Memories of those we left behind, of those whose friendship I enjoyed while they lived, and of the few who are left.

For the Last Time

As I approach my 84th birthday, I am increasingly aware that I would not be alive today if it had not been for the love and care given to me by Esther. Shortly after her 79th birthday and our 49th anniversary, Esther suffered a stroke which was then complicated by pneumonia. She died on July 3, 1983.

Life became terribly lonesome and was made more so at Christmas time when, in response to greetings that I had sent, wives of Jim Fuller and Allison Fishwild sent word that their husbands had died, Jim on November 29 and Fishwild on New Year's Eve. On January 4, I got a telephone call from Hillstead's daughter, Ruth, telling me that my good friend Leonard had died the previous day. Two weeks later, I received a letter from Zephyr Testerman telling me that Ephram had died. I had plans in mind of seeing all of these fellows.

As of today, March 1985, I know of only six of us from "C" Co. who are possibly still about. Jim Higgins in Indiana; Lloyd Anson in San Jose, California; Bill Eckhardt in Ft. Meyers, Florida; Harold Downey in Washington; and possibly Herb Cardner in Illinois.

Esther knew that with the passing of each friend, I felt more and more desolate. Perhaps that is one of the reasons why, even though she was dying and could not speak clearly, Esther managed to say to our daughter, "If something happens to me, who is going to take care of Papa?"

My story, in the main, is from memory. Accuracy of dates and detail relative to the activity of the Division, and the Regiment, in some instances, were checked by referring to the history of the Regiment. I am indebted to Arthur Darios, Supt. of Belleau Wood Cemetery for pamphlets of monuments, cemeteries, and old postcards.

Index